GRAPHIC NONFICTION
SPARTACUS

THE LIFE OF A ROMAN GLADIATOR

by
ROB SHONE & ANITA GANERI

illustrated by
NICK SPENDER

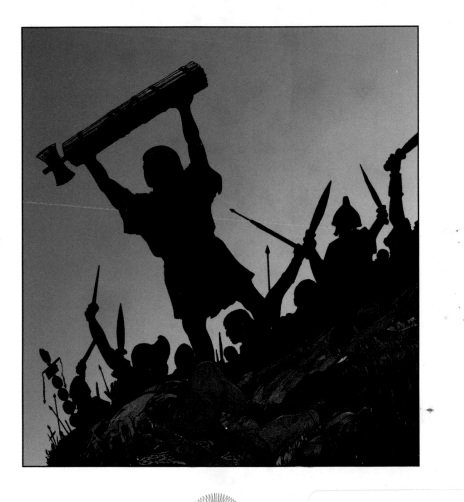

BOOK HOUSE

Designed and produced by
David West 🏃🏃 Children's Books,
7 Princeton Court,
55 Felsham Road,
London, SW15 1 AZ

Editor: Gail Bushnell
Photo Research: Carlotta Cooper

Photo credits:
Page 5 – Robert Harding Picture Library
Page 6 (top) – Mary Evans Picture Library
Pages 7 (both) R. Sheridan, 44 (bottom) Prisma, 45 (top) G. T. Garvey – Ancient Art &
Architecture Collection Ltd.

First published in 2005 by **Book House**,
an imprint of **The Salariya Book Company Ltd**
25 Marlborough Place, Brighton BN1 1UB

Please visit the Salariya Book Company at:
www.salariya.com

HB ISBN 1 904642 87 X
PB ISBN 1 904642 88 8

Visit our website at **www.book-house.co.uk**
for free electronic versions of:
You wouldn't want to be an Egyptian Mummy!
You wouldn't want to be a Roman Gladiator!
Avoid joining Shackleton's Polar Expedition!

Due to the changing nature of internet links, the Salariya Book Company has
developed an online list of websites related to the subject of this book. This site is
updated regularly. Please use this link to access the list:
http://wwwbook-house.co.uk/gnf/spar

A catalogue record for this book is available from the British Library.

Printed on paper from sustainable forests.

Manufactured in China.

CONTENTS

WHO'S WHO

Spartacus (c. 109-71 BC) A Thracian slave and gladiator who led a rebellion against the Romans from 73-71 BC. After many victories, he was finally defeated by Crassus.

Crixus (died 72 B.C.) A gladiator from Gaul and one of Spartacus's deputies. He was killed by the Romans.

Marcus Licinius Crassus (112-53 B.C.) A very wealthy Roman general and politician. With Rome's other top generals fighting abroad, Crassus was sent to do battle with Spartacus and put down the slave rebellion.

Lentulus Batiatus (*dates unknown*) Nothing is known of Lentulus except that he ran a training school for gladiators in Capua, in southern Italy.

Marcus Porcius (*dates unknown*) A local politician from Pompeii, he paid half of the money for an amphitheatre to be built there in 80 BC.

Marcus Tullius Cicero (106-43 BC) A Roman politician, writer, and lawyer, Cicero was famous for his powerful speeches. Many were written down and tell us a great deal about life in Rome.

ROME AND THE REPUBLIC

Map labels:
THE ALPS

Mutina

N / W / E / S (compass)

Tiber R.

ROME

PICENUM

ADRIATIC SEA

Capua

Mt. Vesuvius

Pompeii

Nuceria

CAMPANIA

Brundisium

Thurii

SICILY

BRUTTIUM

Rhegium

MEDITERRANEAN SEA

*I*n the first century BC, Rome conquered the region of the Mediterranean Sea and became its greatest power. Uprisings were quickly put down, to warn other countries not to threaten Rome. Against Rome's power, the gladiator Spartacus led a slave rebellion that shook Rome to the core.

EARLY ROME

Rome began as a group of villages built on seven hills along the River Tiber in Italy. Over time, the villages grew richer and joined together as one town. According to legend, the city of Rome was founded in 753 BC by twin brothers, Romulus and Remus. Until 509 BC, early Rome was ruled by kings. Then King Tarquin the Proud was driven out and Rome became a republic.

SPARTACUS'S ROUTE

73 BC route
72 BC route
71 BC route

The map above shows the routes taken by Spartacus and his slave army in their rebellion against the Romans. The gladiator school where Spartacus trained was at Capua.

GAUL

SPAIN

THRACE

ITALY

GREECE

CILICIA

CARTHAGE

MEDITERRANEAN SEA

AFRICA

EGYPT

ROME IN 100 BC

By 100 BC, Rome had conquered many of the lands around the Mediterranean Sea, including Carthage and Greece.

HOME OF THE SENATE

The Forum was a central part of Roman life. It was a group of buildings that served as a market-place and a meeting place for the Senate.

THE ROMAN REPUBLIC

The Roman republic was governed by a group of officials, called the Senate. The Senate started with 100 senators, but it later had 600. Roman citizens voted each year to elect the senators. Senate affairs and the Roman army were managed by two *consuls*, the most important government officials. They served in office for one year. Other top officials included eight *praetors* who acted mainly as judges in the law courts and four *adiles* who looked after public buildings and organised public games.

EXPANSION OF ROME

By 264 BC, Rome had defeated its Italian neighbours and begun its overseas conquest. The western Mediterranean was controlled by the Carthaginians. The city of Carthage on the north African coast was the centre of a great trading empire. In 264 BC, a series of wars, called the Punic Wars, broke out between Rome and Carthage. Rome beat the Carthaginians and seized their lands. Wars with other powerful states followed. By 50 BC, most of the Mediterranean had fallen to Rome.

GLADIATORS AND THE GAMES

THE AMPHITHEATRE AT POMPEII
The amphitheatre at Pompeii was the first to be built in Italy. It held 20,000 people.

In Roman times, people flocked to the public games that were paid for by the government or wealthy citizens. Though gory, the gladiator fights were hugely popular. They were displays of courage and strength, qualities that the Roman greatly admired.

THE GAMES' BEGINNINGS

Gladiator fights were originally held as part of a funeral to honour a dead person's memory. They were put on by the dead person's family. The first contest in Rome took place in 264 BC, when three pairs of slaves fought in the market-place. Later, special buildings called amphitheatres were built for the games.

GLADIATORS

Gladiators were mostly criminals, slaves, and prisoners of war. They were trained in special gladiator schools. A successful gladiator might win his freedom. But most had short, brutal lives. They only expected to fight two or three times in the arena before they were killed.

TO LIVE OR DIE?

Gladiators usually fought to the death. A wounded fighter could often ask the crowd to decide if he lived or died.

ANIMALS IN THE ARENA

The gladiators fought in the afternoon and were the main attraction at the games. The entertainment began in the morning, with a procession of gladiators, dancers, and musicians. Next came the wild beast shows. Animals were let loose in the arena to fight each other or attack unarmed prisoners. Wealthy Romans spent vast sums of money shipping beasts such as tigers, bears, and rhinoceroses back to Rome to fight.

BEAST HUNTS
Some animals were put in the arena to be hunted by special gladiators called bestiari. *Thousands of people and animals were killed.*

DAILY SLAVES
Slaves had to look after their masters day and night. In the wall painting above, the slaves are serving their masters at a banquet.

A SLAVE'S LIFE
Rome relied heavily on slave labour. Some slaves were owned by rich Romans. The government also owned slaves. Most of Spartacus's rebel army was made up of runaway slaves who joined the gladiators. Many of the slaves had been prisoners of war and had useful military experience.

TYPES OF GLADIATOR
To make the contest even more exciting, fights were held between different types of gladiators. For example, a retiarius, *armed with a trident and net, might be matched against a* murmillo, *armed with a sword and shield.*

Retiarius   Secutor   Murmillo

SPARTACUS

THE LIFE OF A ROMAN GLADIATOR

73 BC IT IS MORNING IN THE TOWN OF POMPEII. THE STREETS ARE UNUSUALLY EMPTY.

OR NEARLY EMPTY...

HURRY UP OR WE'LL MISS THE OPENING PARADE! ARE YOU SURE YOU'VE GOT YOUR TICKET?

YES, UNCLE.

FIRST GAMES, EH? EXCITED?

WELL...

NERVOUS? DON'T WORRY. YOU'LL **LOVE** IT!

SOMEONE ELSE IS IN A HURRY.

YES, DRUSILLA. I'M WELL **AWARE** OF WHAT **CICERO** THINKS.

HE HATES THE GAMES AS MUCH AS YOU DO.

BUT **NOT LIKING** THE GAMES IS SO **UNROMAN!** THE GAMES ARE A SYMBOL OF ROME'S **GREAT POWER** AND **STRENGTH.**

OUT OF THE WAY!

OOF!

CAREFUL, YOU OAF, OR YOU'LL BE CLEANING THE FLOORS USING YOUR OWN SKIN AS A CLOTH!

YOU SEE, THE GAMES SHOW US WHAT IT IS TO BE A ROMAN.

HEY! WATCH YOURSELF!

11

THE AFTERNOON'S ENTERTAINMENT...

CUPIDO? HE'S **PATHETIC!** LOOK AT HIM, FIGHTING BY NUMBERS. SLASH, TWO, THREE! THRUST, TWO, THREE! PATHETIC!

SIXTY SESTERCES ON THE RETIARIUS! WHO'LL TAKE IT?

UH, OH, **TROUBLE.** THE **NUCERIANS** ARE HERE.

CUPIDO! CUPIDO! OOH, ISN'T HE GORGEOUS?

COOEE! CUPIDO! GIVE US A WAVE!

DONE!

I THINK HE'S TOO BUSY TO WAVE AT THE MOMENT, LADIES.

IN THE ARENA, A **SECUTOR** FIGHTS A **RETIARIUS**...

THE RETIARIUS SURRENDERS.

BENEATH THE STANDS "MERCURY" AND "CHARON" TALK...

I **HATE** THIS JOB! PEOPLE DON'T RECOGNISE YOU UNDER ALL THAT PAINT, BUT I'M SICK OF BEING **FOLLOWED** BY KIDS IN THE STREET, CALLING ME NAMES. WE ROMANS CAN BE SO CRUEL AT TIMES!

YEAH, YEAH. LIFE'S TOUGH. IS MY BEARD ON RIGHT?

BY EARLY EVENING, THE GAMES ARE OVER.

I THINK THAT ALL WENT RATHER WELL, DRUSILLA, DEAR. MARCUS PORCIUS IS INTERESTED IN MY LITTLE BUSINESS VENTURE. AND YOUR MOOD CERTAINLY PICKED UP DURING THE AFTERNOON.

YES, I DID FIND SOME OF THE CONTESTS **INTERESTING**. WHO WAS THAT TALL, BLOND RETIARIUS? AURIUS? HE WAS **VERY** INTERESTING!

DRUSILLA! I'M TAKING YOU HOME, RIGHT NOW!

BUT MARCUS PORCIUS IS NOT SO HAPPY...

IT'S A **DISASTER!** THE CROWD EVEN BOOED ME. TO THINK OF ALL THE MONEY IT COST AND I'LL PROBABLY NOT GET A **SINGLE** VOTE TO SHOW FOR IT. THE LIONS WERE **OLD** AND ALMOST **TOOTHLESS** AND NEARLY ALL THE FIGHTS WERE **DULL** AND **BORING!** AND I KNOW WHO'S TO BLAME — THAT MISERABLE WORM, **LENTULUS BATIATUS,** THE LANISTA! I HATE GLADIATOR OWNERS!

BUT **SURELY**, MARCUS, YOU AND MANY OF YOUR FRIENDS **OWN** GLADIATORS. WHY IS LENTULUS SO **DIFFERENT?**

IT'S NOT THE **SAME.** HE'S A PROFESSIONAL OWNER! WE'RE IN IT FOR THE **FUN!**

OUTSIDE, PEOPLE MAKE THEIR WAY HOME...

WELL, BOY, WHAT DID YOU MAKE OF YOUR FIRST GAMES? IT WASN'T A **CLASSIC,** I GRANT YOU. WHAT IT NEEDED WAS AN **INVENTIVE** TOUCH.

ARE YOU ALRIGHT? YOU'RE VERY **QUIET.**

STILL, I THINK YOU'LL MAKE...

...A GOOD **ROMAN.**

SPARTACUS BEGINS TO FORM A PLAN OF ESCAPE...

...HE WATCHES...

...AND LISTENS...

...SEARCHING OUT THE WEAK SPOTS.

FINALLY, HE IS READY.

IS EVERYONE IN, CRIXUS?

YES.

WE GO TONIGHT. YOU ALL KNOW WHAT TO DO.

SNOK

YOU STUPID OX, CRIXUS! TAKE HIM TO THE HOSPITAL.

IN THE HOSPITAL, SECURITY IS NOT TIGHT. WHY BOTHER TO GUARD SICK MEN SO CLOSELY?

COME ON!

THE REBELS HEAD OUT INTO THE COUNTRYSIDE. THEY CAUSE *PANIC* AMONG THE LOCAL PEOPLE.

DRUSILLA, IT'S HARDLY **MY** FAULT ALL OUR SLAVES HAVE RUN AWAY. I DIDN'T START THE TROUBLE. BESIDES WE'LL FEEL MUCH SAFER IN **ROME.**

I KNOW, BUT **LOOK AT MY HAIR!** THERE WAS NO ONE TO COMB IT FOR ME THIS MORNING AND NO ONE TO COOK BREAKFAST. I'M SO **HUNGRY!** **AND** I HAD TO DO ALL MY OWN PACKING!

MY ARMS ARE STILL ACHING FROM ALL **YOUR** PACKING!

I'VE **ALWAYS** HAD SLAVES AND I HATE **NOT** HAVING THEM. I FEEL SO **POOR!**

I'M BEGINNING TO THINK I SHOULD HAVE LEFT YOU BEHIND FOR YOUR **GLADIATOR BOYFRIEND!**

SUETONIUS PAULINUS! YOU CAN BE SO **CRUDE** AT TIMES!

OTHERS ARE TRYING TO FLEE...

BUT UNCLE, I THOUGHT YOU SAID THAT A GOOD ROMAN ISN'T AFRAID OF ANYTHING, NOT EVEN DEATH.

AND A FAT LOT OF GOOD THIS ROMAN WOULD BE LYING IN A DITCH WITH HIS THROAT CUT. NOW GET ON THE CART, BOY. **WE'RE OFF!**

IN ROME, THE SENATE TAKES A **CALMER** VIEW...

I SEE NO NEED FOR **ALARM.** WHAT HARM CAN THIS RAGGED ARMY OF THIEVES AND CUTTHROATS DO TO THE **MIGHT** OF ROME?

TRUE, OUR FINEST GENERALS AND BEST LEGIONS ARE **ABROAD.** BUT THE TROOPS LEFT AT HOME SHOULD BE MORE THAN ENOUGH TO DESTROY THIS **MOB.**

SOON THEY WILL ALL WISH THEY HAD **DIED** IN THE ARENA.

PRAETOR CLAUDIUS GLABER IS GIVEN THE TASK OF SORTING OUT THE TROUBLE IN POMPEII...

WE MUST BE **CAREFUL**, PRAETOR. THE MEN ARE WILLING BUT THEY ARE NEW RECRUITS.

CENTURION, I HAVE 3,000 MEN AGAINST A HANDFUL OF **DISORGANISED** SLAVES. WHAT IS THERE TO FEAR?

SIR! NEWS FROM VESUVIUS.

ON THE LOWER SLOPES OF MOUNT VESUVIUS...

THEY ARE ON THE TOP OF THE MOUNTAIN. THE **ONLY** WAY DOWN IS ALONG THAT PATH.

EXCELLENT! SOONER OR LATER, THEY WILL HAVE TO COME THROUGH THAT NARROW PASS. WHEN THEY **DO**, WE'LL BE **WAITING**!

THE GLADIATORS' CAMP...

WE'RE **TRAPPED**! WE'LL NEVER GET DOWN THAT WAY. WE'LL ALL BE **KILLED**...

...AND THE CLIFFS ON EITHER SIDE OF US ARE TOO **STEEP** TO CLIMB.

25

SHORTLY, SLAVES ARE AT WORK ON A QUIET COUNTRY VILLA...

?

THE REBELS! RUN!

SPARTACUS'S SLAVE ARMY MARCHES THROUGH CAMPANIA...

...TAKING ANYTHING THEY WANT.

GET ALL THE HORSES AND ANY WEAPONS AND ARMOUR YOU CAN FIND.

THE GAMES ARE OVER. 'CHARON' AND 'MERCURY' ARE ON THE ROAD LOOKING FOR NEW JOBS...

THE GAMES **ARE** THEATRE. THE SMELL OF THE **BLOOD**, THE ROAR OF THE **LIONS!**

YOU CAN'T **BLAME** THEM, THE WAY WE ROMANS **TREAT** THEM.

I WON'T NEED THESE FOR A WHILE. NO GAMES MEANS NO 'CHARON' OR 'MERCURY'.

IT'S BACK TO THE THEATRE FOR US THEN.

THERE GOES THE SLAVE ARMY, SPOILING THINGS FOR EVERYONE.

WELL, THEY SEEM TO BE GOING **SOUTH**. WE'LL GO NORTH.

THE SENATE STAYS CALM AS IT HEARS THE NEWS FROM VESUVIUS. ANOTHER ARMY IS SENT OUT. IT CARRIES THE *FASCES*, AN AXE WRAPPED IN A BUNDLE OF REEDS. THIS IS THE SYMBOL OF THE SENATE'S *AUTHORITY* AND OF ROME'S *MIGHT* AND *POWER*.

THE ROMAN ARMY AND THE REBELS MEET...

DESPITE ALL ITS TRAINING, THE ROMAN ARMY IS NOT PREPARED FOR THE REBELS' FEROCIOUS ATTACK. THE FASCES ARE TAKEN.

SPARTACUS AND HIS ARMY HAVE WON THEIR FIRST VICTORY AGAINST ROME IN OPEN BATTLE.

WHAT ARE YOUR PLANS, SPARTACUS?

IT WILL SOON BE WINTER, CRIXUS. WE MUST FIND SOMEWHERE TO CAMP UNTIL THE SPRING. AFTER THAT, WE **HEAD NORTH**.

TO ROME?

NO, TO THE **ALPS**. WE'LL CROSS THE MOUNTAINS INTO GAUL, AND **HOME!**

SPARTACUS, WE HAVE **SHOWN** THE SENATE THAT THEIR ARMIES ARE NO MATCH FOR US. WHY STOP? WHY NOT GO TO ROME AND **BRING DOWN** THE REPUBLIC ITSELF? THINK OF **THE RICHES** TO BE HAD THERE.

ROME IS JUST SLEEPING. WE CAUGHT IT BY SURPRISE, THAT'S ALL. BUT IT WILL **SOON WAKE UP** AND COME AFTER US. BY THAT TIME, WE MUST BE FAR AWAY FROM ROME, AND ITALY.

THEN WE GAULS AND GERMANS WILL GO OUR OWN WAY.

SPARTACUS LEADS HIS ARMY OF 70,000 TO THURII IN THE FAR SOUTH. THEY WILL STAY HERE FOR THE WINTER. DISCIPLINE SOON BECOMES A **PROBLEM...**

THEY'VE BEEN FIGHTING OVER THEIR **LOOT**.

WHAT GOOD WILL **GOLD** BE TO THEM WHEN THEY FACE A ROMAN LEGION? HALF THE MEN DON'T HAVE WEAPONS OR ARMOUR.

FROM NOW ON, ONLY IRON AND COPPER WILL BE ALLOWED INTO CAMP. FIND SOME BLACKSMITHS. WE HAVE **WEAPONS** TO MAKE.

MEANWHILE, CRIXUS AND HIS GAULS AND GERMANS ARE LIVING THE GOOD LIFE.

THE SPRING OF 72 BC FINDS THEM NORTH OF THURII.

CRIXUS DOES NOT KNOW IT YET, BUT ROME HAS SENT A NEW ARMY MADE UP OF FOUR LEGIONS TO FIND AND KILL HIM.

WHILE CRIXUS AND HIS REBELS EAT AND DRINK, CONSUL GELLIUS PUBLICOLA AND TWO OF THE LEGIONS ARE MOVING CLOSE TO CRIXUS'S CAMP...

...VERY CLOSE.

THE ROMANS KILL CRIXUS AND 20,000 OF HIS MEN.

29

SPARTACUS HAS LEFT THURII AND GONE NORTH. HE HAS HEARD OF CRIXUS'S DEATH AND WANTS TO **DESTROY THE ROMANS!** MEANWHILE, CONSUL CORNELIUS LENTULUS CLODIANUS PREPARES HIS TWO LEGIONS TO FACE SPARTACUS AND HIS REBELS.

HERE THEY COME. I DON'T EXPECT THIS TO TAKE TOO LONG. SEE! THEIR LEFT WING IS ALREADY FALLING BACK.

LOOK! ARE THEY SUPPOSED TO HAVE HORSEMEN? WE HAVE NONE, DO WE?

WHAT?

YOU FOOL! THEY DON'T JUST HAVE HORSEMEN, THEY HAVE A **CAVALRY!** SOUND THE **RETREAT!** THEY'LL HAVE MY **HEAD** IN ROME FOR THIS, IF I'VE STILL GOT ONE!

IN MEMORY OF CRIXUS, SPARTACUS HOLDS GAMES. THE 300 ROMAN PRISONERS ARE THE GLADIATORS. THEY ARE FORCED TO FIGHT EACH OTHER TO THE DEATH.

HOW DID YOU MANAGE TO TRICK THE ROMANS, SPARTACUS? IT'S AS IF YOU THINK LIKE THEM.

I WAS ONE OF THEM ONCE. I SERVED IN THEIR ARMY AS A SOLDIER.

WHAT HAPPENED?

I RAN AWAY BUT THEY CAUGHT ME AND MADE ME A GLADIATOR. YES, I KNOW THE ROMANS.

MARCHING NORTH, SPARTACUS BRUSHES ASIDE AN ATTACK BY A ROMAN ARMY AT PICENUM AND ANOTHER ATTACK AT MUTINA.

BY EARLY AUTUMN OF 72 BC, THE ROAD NORTH IS CLEAR AND SPARTACUS CAN **ESCAPE** OVER THE ALPS. BUT **FEW** WISH TO FOLLOW HIM.

SPARTACUS, WE **CAN'T** GO. SOME OF US HAVE BEEN HERE AS SLAVES FOR YEARS. WHEN THE ROMANS CAME, THEY BURNED MY VILLAGE. MY WIFE AND CHILDREN ARE **DEAD**, OR SLAVES THEMSELVES FOR ALL I KNOW. I HAVE NO HOME.

THERE ARE OVER **100,000** OF US, MEN, WOMEN, AND CHILDREN. HOW ARE WE **ALL** TO GET OVER THE MOUNTAINS? DO **YOU** KNOW A WAY? BESIDES, WE WON'T EVEN REACH THE ALPS BEFORE WINTER.

WE'VE **BEATEN** THE ROMANS AT EVERY TURN. WHO'S TO SAY WE CAN'T DO IT AGAIN AND AGAIN?

IF I AM TO DIE, THEN LET IT BE CLUTCHING A SWORD IN ONE HAND AND A **ROMAN'S THROAT** IN THE OTHER!

YES! TO ROME! LET'S BURN THE WHOLE PLACE DOWN!

BUT NOT BEFORE WE'VE MADE OFF WITH ALL ITS **GOLD!**

MAYBE YOU'RE RIGHT. IT'S NOT THE TIME TO GO NORTH. IF WE TURN SOUTH, WE MEET ALMOST CERTAIN DEATH. BUT AT LEAST WE WILL DIE AS **FREE MEN!**

33

IN ROME, POLITICIAN MARCUS CICERO IS ENTERTAINING GUESTS...

THEY'VE BEEN **FRIGHTENING** THE COUNTRY FOR NEARLY **TWO YEARS!** THERE'S HARDLY AN ESTATE IN CENTRAL ITALY THAT THOSE THIEVES HAVEN'T VISITED! AND THINK OF ALL THE SLAVES THEY'VE **FREED** AND ALL THE TREASURES THEY'VE **TAKEN!**

IT WOULD SEEM WE ARE **POWERLESS** TO STOP THEM, CICERO! THEY HAVE TURNED US ALL INTO **LAUGHING STOCKS.**

WE **COULD** CALL **POMPEY** BACK FROM FIGHTING THE SPANISH REBELS.

HE'D LIKE NOTHING MORE THAN TO MARCH AN ARMY INTO ITALY. ONCE HE'D DEALT WITH THE REBELS, HE'D KEEP ON MARCHING – **STRAIGHT INTO ROME!**

POMPEY? HE'S MORE **DANGEROUS** THAN THOSE GLADIATOR THUGS!

WE NEED TO FIND SOMEONE **LESS HEADSTRONG** BUT JUST AS FIERCE AND EXPERIENCED.

WHAT ABOUT **MARCUS CRASSUS?**

MARCUS CRASSUS? YES. HE'S **CLEVER** AND HE HAS LED SOLDIERS IN BATTLE. HE IS ALSO VERY **RICH** AND COULD EVEN **AFFORD TO PAY** FOR AN ARMY.

IN THE AUTUMN OF 72 BC THE SENATE APPOINTS MARCUS CRASSUS OVERALL COMMANDER OF THE ARMY IN ITALY. HE HAS SIX NEW LEGIONS UNDER HIM AS WELL AS THE CONSULS' FOUR LEGIONS.

MY PLAN IS TO **WAIT** FOR MY FULL FORCE. WE'LL THEN **PUSH** THE REBELS SOUTH, **AWAY** FROM ROME.

MEANWHILE, TAKE TWO LEGIONS, MUMMIUS, AND FOLLOW THE REBELS.

YOU ARE NOT TO ENGAGE THEM IN BATTLE.

MUMMIUS AND HIS LEGIONS SPOT THE ENEMY...

FORM THE MEN INTO BATTLE LINES.

BUT SIR, OUR ORDERS!

CRASSUS IS A CAUTIOUS FOOL. THEY ARE NOTHING BUT A BAND OF **BEGGARS AND OUTLAWS.**

THE ROMANS ARE **BADLY BEATEN.** PART OF THE ROMAN ARMY FLEES.

CRASSUS IS **FURIOUS** WITH MUMMIUS. AS **PUNISHMENT,** THE TROOPS THAT FLED ARE **DECIMATED.** THIS MEANS ONE MAN OUT OF TEN IS CHOSEN BY LOT AND **CLUBBED TO DEATH** BY HIS FELLOW SOLDIERS.

THEY WILL LEARN TO **FEAR ME MORE** THAN THEY FEAR THE **REBELS.**

CRASSUS'S ARMY GRADUALLY FORCES THE REBELS SOUTH TO BRUTTIUM.

THEY HAVE **NOWHERE** TO GO NOW. I WANT TO **KEEP** IT THAT WAY.

THE ROMANS BUILD A WALL AND A DITCH. IT TRAPS THE REBELS IN SOUTHERN ITALY.

IT STRETCHES FROM COAST TO COAST.

MEANWHILE, AT THE SOUTHERN TIP OF MAINLAND ITALY...

WE JUST NEED TO GET TO **SICILY**. IT WON'T TAKE MUCH TO SPARK A **NEW REBELLION**.

SPARTACUS HIRES CILICIAN PIRATES TO FERRY THEM TO SICILY.*

HAVE WE GOT A DEAL?

HAVE YOU GOT THE GOLD?

LATER...

DO YOU REALLY MEAN TO HELP THESE THIEVES?

HALF NOW, THE REST IN SICILY.

YOU HAVE A DEAL.

*CILICIAN PIRATES (FROM MODERN-DAY TURKEY) CAPTURED TRADING SHIPS AND RAIDED PORTS THROUGHOUT THE MEDITERRANEAN SEA.

I'D ENJOY WATCHING THE ROMANS SQUIRM A LITTLE! THEY PUT UP WITH US FOR THE MOMENT. BUT IF THEY FOUND OUT WE HELPED THE SLAVES, THEY WOULD NOT BE SO FORGIVING. STILL, WE HAVE THE SLAVES' MONEY. WE SAIL TONIGHT, FOR HOME!

BY MORNING, THE PIRATE SHIPS HAVE GONE.

BACK AT THE CAMP...

WHAT ARE YOU DOING?

WE CAUGHT THIS ROMAN SPY. WE THOUGHT WE'D HAVE A BIT OF FUN!

ROME WILL NOT SEE IT LIKE THAT.

CRUCIFIED? AN INNOCENT ROMAN CITIZEN? A SHAMEFUL DEATH – SHAMEFUL FOR ROME!

WHERE WILL THESE BARBARIAN DEVILS STOP? ON THE HILLS OF **ROME?**

DO YOU KNOW HOW MANY GLADIATORS, LET ALONE SLAVES, ARE CURRENTLY IN ROME? **THOUSANDS!** WHAT DO YOU THINK WOULD HAPPEN IF THEY ALL CAUGHT THIS **FREEDOM DISEASE?**

WE MUST SEND FOR POMPEY AND CALL LICINIUS LUCULLUS AND HIS LEGIONS BACK FROM MACEDONIA IN THE EAST. THE DANGER TO ROME IS TOO GREAT.

BUT SPARTACUS'S MEN NEED FOOD AND SUPPLIES. THEY MUST BREAK THROUGH THE ROMAN WALL. THEY HAVE TESTED THE ROMAN GUARDS ALL ALONG ITS VAST LENGTH, LOOKING FOR WEAK POINTS. NOW, THEY DARE NOT FAIL.

WHAT A FILTHY NIGHT! WHEN DO WE GO OFF DUTY?

ABOUT AN HOUR.

DID YOU HEAR SOMETHING?

IT'S JUST THE WIND.

NO, THERE IT GOES AGAIN!

IT IS 71 BC. SPARTACUS FLEES EAST AS FAST AS HE CAN. HE HOPES TO GET TO *BRUNDISIUM* ON THE COAST. THEN BAD NEWS ARRIVES. LUCULLUS AND HIS ARMY ARE BACK FROM MACEDONIA AND HAVE LANDED ON THE EAST COAST. THE WAY FORWARD IS *BLOCKED*.

WE HAVE AN ARMY IN *FRONT* OF US, CRASSUS CHASING FROM BEHIND, AND POMPEY TO THE *NORTH*. WE CAN DO NO MORE. WE *STAND* AND *FIGHT*.

IN SOUTHERN CAMPANIA SPARTACUS'S ARMY TURNS AROUND, FORMS INTO BATTLE LINES, AND WAITS FOR CRASSUS.

AT LAST! THEY WISH TO FIGHT IN OPEN BATTLE.

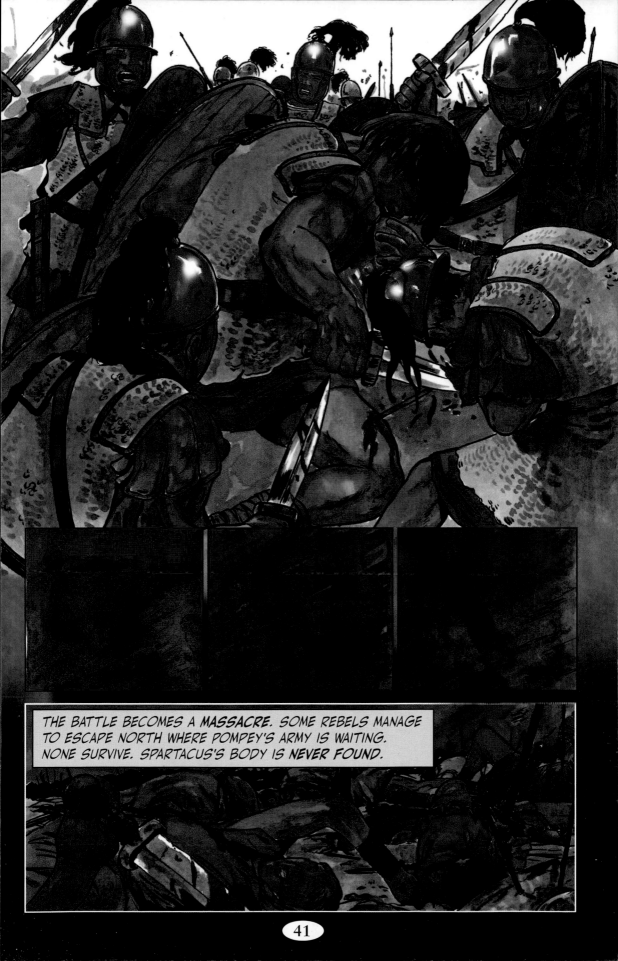

THE BATTLE BECOMES A *MASSACRE*. SOME REBELS MANAGE TO ESCAPE NORTH WHERE POMPEY'S ARMY IS WAITING. NONE SURVIVE. SPARTACUS'S BODY IS *NEVER FOUND*.

THE ROMANS TAKE 6,000 REBEL PRISONERS. THEY ARE **CRUCIFIED** ALONG THE **APPIAN WAY**, WHICH RUNS FROM CAPUA TO ROME. ONE CAPTIVE HANGS EVERY 27 METRES FOR 320 KM.

ROME FINDS IT HAS NEW PROBLEMS. BOTH POMPEY AND CRASSUS ARE CLAIMING VICTORY OVER THE REBELS. NEITHER WILL LET HIS ARMY GO. IF A SOLUTION IS NOT FOUND, IT WILL MEAN **CIVIL WAR**...

FAMILY! THEY WERE LIKE **FAMILY** TO ME, GERMANICUS! NOW THE GOOD NAME LENTULUS BATIATUS ISN'T WORTH A LEAD SESTERCE. WE CAN'T STAY IN ITALY.

LET POMPEY HAVE HIS VICTORY PARADE THROUGH ROME, CRASSUS, NOT FOR HIS SMALL PART IN DEFEATING THE REBELS BUT FOR HIS SPANISH CAMPAIGN. AFTER ALL, WHERE IS THE GLORY IN BEATING A FEW THOUSAND CRIMINALS? STAND YOUR ARMY DOWN AND FORM AN ALLIANCE WITH HIM. ROME WILL BE **ETERNALLY GRATEFUL TO YOU.**

KERLIP KERLOP

WISE WORDS. I WILL GAIN MORE FOR SEEMING TO BE A PEACEMAKER THAN A WARMONGER. I CAN SEE YOU MAY RISE TO GREAT HEIGHTS ONE DAY, **GAIUS JULIUS CAESAR.**

I'VE HEARD THE GAMES ARE POPULAR IN THE PROVINCES. PERHAPS WE SHOULD GO TO SPAIN, OR EVEN AFRICA? WE'D BE CLOSE TO A READY SUPPLY OF SLAVES AND WILD BEASTS AND FREE FROM INTERFERING BUSY-BODIES. HMM, **AFRICA!**

BY THE AUTUMN, LIFE IS BACK TO NORMAL. MEANWHILE, IN THE AMPHITHEATRE AT POMPEII...

SO, HERE WE ARE AGAIN FOR ANOTHER DAY OF FUN, THRILLS, AND SPILLS.

DO YOU THINK THE GAMES HAVE A **FUTURE?**

MARCUS PORCIUS!

OF COURSE! LISTEN TO THAT ROAR. DEATH SELLS.

AFTER THE REVOLT

Although Spartacus's uprising was finally crushed, it had been a warning to the Romans. The Senate had not taken the rebels seriously enough and many Romans had been killed in the fighting. Rome was determined that this sort of threat to its power would never happen again.

The Colosseum
Opened in AD 80,
the Colosseum
in Rome was
the greatest
amphitheatre in
the Roman Empire.
This vast building had
room for about
50,000
people.

AFTERMATH

After Spartacus's uprising, several other groups of gladiators tried to rebel. These revolts did not last long and were quickly put down by the Romans. To make sure that the revolts stopped, the Romans applied stricter discipline at the gladiator schools. The gladiators were closely supervised and the stores of weapons carefully guarded.

AN UNEASY PEACE

After putting down the slave rebellion, Pompey and Crassus joined forces and demanded to be made *consuls*. They were elected in 70 BC. In 60 BC, Pompey and Crassus formed an alliance with Julius Caesar against their political rivals, a group of senators called *optimates*. Caesar was elected consul in 59 BC.

JULIUS CAESAR

Julius Caesar (c. 100-44 BC) was a brilliant soldier and politician. Caesar led his armies into Spain, Gaul and Britain before returning to Rome to take power.

CIVIL WAR

In 53 BC, Crassus was killed in battle and the alliance began to break up. With Caesar away in Gaul or modern-day France, the Senate persuaded Pompey to become consul. The *optimates* were worried that Caesar would return to Rome and challenge their authority. Civil war broke out between Caesar and Pompey, who was backed by the *optimates*. In 49 BC, however, Caesar led his army into Rome and seized power. Over the next few years, he defeated Pompey's armies in Spain, Greece, and Africa.

THE END OF THE REPUBLIC

Following his victories, Caesar was made dictator for life. Caesar introduced popular social reforms, but many senators felt that he threatened their power. He was murdered on 15th March, 44 BC. Civil wars broke out and the republic ended. In 27 BC, Caesar's adopted son, Octavian, defeated his rivals to become leader of the Roman world. He took the name 'Augustus' and became the first Roman emperor.

POMPEY THE GREAT
The powerful Roman general Pompey (106-48 BC), was called back from fighting in Spain to help Crassus crush Spartacus's rebellion. Pompey was later elected consul.

SPARTACUS IN HISTORY
The information we have about Spartacus comes mainly from two Greek writers, Appian and Plutarch. They describe Spartacus as a villain and the enemy of Rome. Today, however, many people view Spartacus as a hero and freedom fighter. Sports like foxhunting and bullfighting are modern-day reminders of the Roman games.

GLOSSARY

alliance An agreement to work together.

amphitheatre A circular or oval building in which gladiator fights were held.

Appian Way The first major road to be built in Rome. It ran from Rome to Capua.

arena A large area used for sports or entertainment.

cavalry Soldiers who fight on horseback.

centurion An officer in the Roman army who commanded a unit of around 80 men.

Charon The boatman who ferried people's souls across the River Styx to the Underworld.

consul The most senior official in the Roman government. Two consuls were elected each year.

crucify To put someone to death by nailing to a cross.

decimate To select by lot and kill every tenth man; to destroy a large part of something.

discipline Control over the way someone thinks or behaves.

execution The killing of someone for a crime.

Gauls People who lived in what is now France.

legion A 5,000-man unit of the Roman army.

massacre The brutal killing of a large number of people.

murmillo A gladiator who fought with a sword and shield.

Nucerians People from the city of Nuceria, east of Pompeii.

oath A serious, formal promise.

praetor A senior official in the Roman government.

province An outlying area of a country, away from the centre of population.

ration To give out in limited amounts.

rebellion A struggle against the people in charge of something.

recruits People who have recently joined an army or organisation.

republic A country or state in which the people elect representatives who manage the government.

retiarius A gladiator who fought with a net and a trident.

secutor A gladiator who fought with a sword and shield, often chasing his opponent, who would normally be a *retiarius*.

Senate The group of officials which governed Rome. These officials were called senators.

sesterces Units of Roman currency.

sponsor Someone who gives money to support the work of others.

Thracian A person from Thrace, or what is now Bulgaria.

trident A long, three-pronged spear.